BOULEZ

Oxford Studies of Composers

Oxford Studies of Composers (16)

BOULEZ

PAUL GRIFFITHS

1478
1978

London

OXFORD UNIVERSITY PRESS

NEW YORK   MELBOURNE

1978

Oxford University Press, Walton Street, Oxford OX2 6DP

OXFORD LONDON GLASGOW NEW YORK
TORONTO MELBOURNE WELLINGTON CAPE TOWN
IBADAN NAIROBI DAR ES SALAAM LUSAKA
KUALA LUMPUR SINGAPORE JAKARTA HONG KONG TOKYO
DELHI BOMBAY CALCUTTA MADRAS KARACHI

ISBN 0 19 315442 0

© Paul Griffiths 1978

174905

*Printed and bound in Great Britain
at the Scolar Press Ilkley West Yorkshire*

CONTENTS

For Stanley Sadie

PREFACE

ANY study of Pierre Boulez's music is, at this stage in his career, necessarily tentative. Not only is his work still, one hopes, incomplete, but it is also in a state of change. Several of his scores remain as 'works in progress', unfinished many years after their first conception; others have been withdrawn, in some cases to be revised or recomposed. Sufficient example may be provided by his very first composition, *Notations** for piano (1945), which Boulez has suggested he may rework as an orchestral piece.

This essay is, therefore, partial and preliminary, and would have been much more so had it not been for assistance provided by the staff of Universal Edition (London) Ltd and Heugel et Cie (Paris). I would also like to thank Pierre Boulez himself for authenticating my listing of his works.

All music examples are notated at sounding pitch, and are reproduced by kind permission of Universal Edition (London) Ltd. (Exx. 12, 14–17, 19–27, 29, 30, 32–35, 37, 38–44), Heugel et Cie. (Exx. 1, 7–9, 10, 11), and Éditions Musicales Amphion (Exx. 2–6).

---

* This work, unpublished and long unheard, was revived for a performance broadcast by Radio France on 1 July 1978. It is a set of twelve very short pieces, highly diverse in character, often suggesting the influence of Schoenberg's atonal piano writing.

FIRST WORKS

Every creative act implies particular technical and aesthetic principles, yet there can have been few artists who, like Pierre Boulez, have seen the establishment of such principles as an urgent responsibility. Right from the first he has been guided by the need to lay new foundations for the musical 'language', to make coherent order from the revolution of the early part of the twentieth century. 'Our first effort', he has recalled, 'was to seek—perhaps naïvely, but not unhappily so—a grammatical expression which would fix the language in precise ways, and which would fix it for a long time to come.'

This effort had its roots in Messiaen's harmony class at the Paris Conservatoire, which Boulez joined in 1944 at the age of nineteen. He studied with Messiaen only for one academic year, but that was enough to open him to a new world of musical thought. 'It was', in Boulez's own words, 'truly an epoch of searching and liberation. . . . Secretly (or almost so) we learned to have total admiration for names no one spoke of, to know unknown works, led to them by our penetration—meanwhile we proceeded further together. Not only Europe had preference in our investigation; we were taught knowledge of Asia and Africa, so that we abandoned the privilege of 'tradition'. For us they opened an arena in which music was more than just an art object, it was truly a way of life: an unextinguished torch.'

Among the works which Boulez wrote while in Messiaen's class, all subsequently withdrawn, are the *Trois Psalmodies* for piano (1945). The title may suggest an indebtedness to Messiaen, whose then recent *Trois Petites Liturgies* (1944) concludes with a 'Psalmodie de l'ubiquité par amour', but according to Goléa the music relates also to Schoenberg's Three Pieces Op. 11, being 'on the confines of the modal writing dear to Messiaen and of atonality'. Boulez himself has said that when he wrote the work he 'scarcely knew of the existence of serial music but very clearly felt the necessity of atonality'.

His awakening to serialism came later in the same year when he heard René Leibowitz conduct a performance of Schoenberg's Wind Quintet. It is ironic that this should have been the work to introduce Boulez to serial technique, for he soon came to the conclusion that Schoenberg's use of classical forms in serial music was 'the most perfect *misdirection* that could have been offered in contemporary music' (1949). For the moment, however, he was sufficiently impressed to go to Leibowitz for private tuition in serialism, which he immediately began to practise in his composition. He was determined that he would not make Schoenberg's 'mistake', and he looked to Webern as an alternative father of serialism, as 'THE threshold', to quote a later essay. Ignoring the fact that Webern's adherence to established formal schemes was hardly less strict than Schoenberg's, he found that in Webern 'the series immediately took on the aspect of a function of intervals, giving its basic structure to the piece itself'. It would seem that he was attracted by Webern's use of the series to engender all the melodic and harmonic features of a work, so that 'the frontier between the horizontal and the vertical dimension is abolished', and that he recognized in Webern's music a correspondence between the symmetry of the series and the symmetry or canonic form of the work. Yet direct imitation was never to be Boulez's way, and it makes little sense to define his serial technique as 'post-Webernian'. He rejected both the thematic serialism of Schoenberg and the motivic serialism of Webern, extrapolating far beyond both.

This is apparent at once in his first three serial works, the Sonatina for flute and piano, the First Piano Sonata, and the cantata *Le Visage nuptial*, all composed in 1946–7. Patent serial statements are rare in all these pieces: Ex. 1, from the end of the first movement of *Le Visage nuptial*, comes after a mêlée of ramified workings in which it is impossible to follow the serial construction in detail:

Ex. 1

Instead of respecting the integrity of the series, Boulez uses it as a source of smaller units which can be developed independently, as may be seen most readily in the Sonatina.

The series of this work (Ex. 2 shows its first unambiguous statement) contains two appearances of a motif, marked 'x' in the example, consisting of a tritone followed or preceded by a fourth or fifth:

Ex. 2

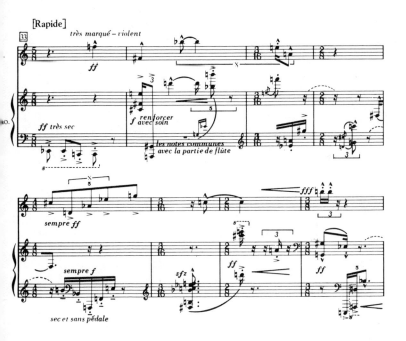

This privileged motif gives the piece one of its most characteristic melodic and harmonic units. Ex. 3, from the closing bars of the single-movement work, displays an emphatic recall of the Ex. 2 flute part in minor ninths (note that in bar 505 Boulez replaces the 'correct' D in the lower part with an E in order to avoid a close repetition):

Ex. 3,

9

Then the 'x' motif is recalled as a chord of G–C♯–A♭, this referring directly to the introduction, and the work ends with the same motif shot into the upper treble.

Another example of this motif's prominence is provided by the 'Tempo scherzando' music, whose skipping little theme (Ex. 4) is constructed from it as shown (note the recollection of this idea in Ex. 3):

Ex. 4

The term 'theme' is indeed appropriate here, for the development of the idea, if capricious, is more blatant than Boulez would later allow. It is worth noting the use of note repetition to give a perky definition to the theme (this technique appears again, though in rather different circumstances, in the Second Piano Sonata) and the prominence of the minor third, an interval foreign to the series.

There are indeed few places in the Sonatina where the music can be analysed in orthodox serial terms. Boulez appears to have been pushing his new-found technique as far as it would go, and in several diverse directions. His usage varies from making the series into a trilling cantus firmus (bars 97–138) to having serial statements in the flute absorbed into an effectively non-serial piano development (as in Ex. 2) or splitting several serial forms into component intervals and then reshuffling them:

Ex. 5

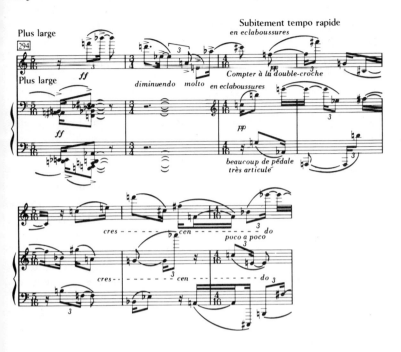

This last passage uses a serial fragment as a periodic call to attention, as at the beginning of the example, but the following three-part counterpoint is deliberately composed as a 'rhythmic development' without thematic reference.

If Schoenberg has been here all but forgotten (and Webern too), his memory remains in some of the piano writing of the Sonatina and in the formal plan of the work. Boulez was greatly impressed by Schoenberg's writing for 'a percussive piano which is at the same time remarkably prone to frenzy', above all in the third piece of Op. 11 and 'Die Kreuze' from *Pierrot lunaire*, this being just one aspect of his preference for the freedom of invention in the pre-serial atonal works of Schoenberg, Berg, and Webern. As far as form is concerned, however, he turned to an earlier composition of Schoenberg's, the First Chamber Symphony, and emulated its synthesis of four movement-types. A slow introduction is followed by an 'allegro' (Ex. 2 comes from the opening of this), a 'slow movement' (the cantus firmus section), a 'scherzo' ('Tempo scherzando'), and a 'finale' where toccata-like motion races the music towards its close. Boulez never tried this again—he quickly grew intolerant of backward glances in matters of form—and yet the balancing of different kinds of musical motion, primitively essayed in the Sonatina, has remained important to his creative thought.

Musical motion, in the sense in which the phrase is used here, concerns not only tempo but also rhythmic character, and the Sonatina is no less wide-ranging in its rhythmic than in its serial conceptions. Boulez had learned from Messiaen, and through him from Stravinsky, to think in terms of rhythmic 'cells', each of a few notes, and he had also taken note of the subtle use of irrational values and grace notes in Varèse and Jolivet. Passages like Exx. 4 and 5 show him following Messiaen quite directly in composing counterpoints of cellular lines, but Ex. 2 is more significant for the future in its free association of cells, its 'rhythmic atonality', so to speak. As Boulez wrote in 1948, speaking of his rhythmic technique, 'the principle of variation and of constant renewal will guide us unpityingly'.

In the First Piano Sonata this 'constant renewal' is raised almost to a general principle, to the extent that continuous change becomes an important factor in the music's momentum. There are now no thematic sections like the 'scherzo' of the Sonatina, nor even any remnants of exact motivic recall such as have been noted in the earlier work. Instead the music is allusively composed on what Boulez has called 'a certain texture of intervals', persistently reinterpreted. The slow sections of the first movement, for instance, are concerned largely with the first five notes of the series (F♯–D–F–E♭–E as they first appear), a chromatic fragment. In the opening bars:

Ex. 6

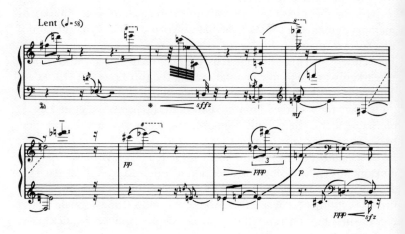

one may note the changes made to the initial pair in five appearances, one of them disguised by a mimicry of rhythm with change of motif (bar 5). Equally significant is the gradual filling in of the chromatic space, which takes place both in the serial segment and in the music: the appearance of an A♮ is delayed until bar 9, and at the end of the movement a high G completes the total after an eleven-note chord which had seemed final. In Boulez's later music this is still a technique of central importance.

The larger structure of the First Sonata depends again on differences in the kind of motion employed. The first movement alternates slow music of intervallic variation (as in Ex. 6) with stiltedly moving faster material, and the two main types in the second and final movement are a supple two-part counterpoint of interlacing, rhythmically divergent lines and a toccata. Unlike that of the Sonatina, whose varied accents had suggested Stravinsky as ancestor, the toccata of the First Sonata is devoid of particular emphases, moving generally in even quavers or semiquavers. It has a static dynamism which is more Asian than European, and it contrasts completely with the pulseless floating of the movement's other music.

It was unlikely that this simple opposition would satisfy Boulez for long, and in the Second Piano Sonata (1947–8) he produced a work in which the variation of motion is very much more subtle. The Second Sonata is also very much more complex than the First: a lost work, the *Symphonie concertante* for piano and orchestra (1947), was apparently a link. Where a two-part texture was normal in the First Sonata, the Second commonly employs three or four strands which Boulez insists are of equal importance. The difference is that between a baroque sonata and the 'Hammerklavier', and one may fairly assume the Second Sonata to have been a consciously Beethovenian assault.

There are four movements, roughly to be described as a sonata allegro, a bi-partite slow movement, a scherzo with three trios, and a finale containing two quasi-fugal developments. The first movement can be considered as elaborating the motifs contained in the serial statement of its first two bars:

Ex. 7

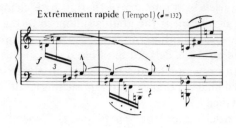

but these are developed in such dense, frenetic counterpoint that their identities become almost annihilated. Ex. 8 shows a not untypical passage from late in the movement where, though it is still possible to descry suggestions of the original motifs (particularly, of course, that with a repeated note), the impression is of a welter of confusion in which one grasps at sporadic half-memories:

Ex. 8

Such tangled counterpoints of cells, which are characteristic of the sonata, are alternated in the first movement with abrupt chordal onslaughts which serve to re-inject the development with energy whenever it shows signs of flagging or comes to a dead end. They themselves strive towards an even quaver motion which, once achieved, is suddenly galloped into triplets before the counterpoint returns 'rapide et violent'.

The slow movement offers some appeasement in its fluid, leisurely progress, interrupted by comments, faster or slower than the prevailing movement, often presented between pauses:

Ex. 9

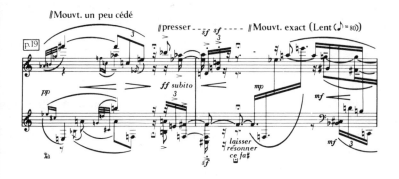

This introduction of musical 'parentheses' was to be developed by Boulez in the mid-fifties, notably in the Third Piano Sonata, and the movement is similarly forward-looking in its large-scale form. The first part, played without interpolated commentary, is repeated in the second part as the underlying thread of what Boulez calls a 'troped' development, relating his technique to the medieval practice of putting insertions into plainsong. However, only at the end of the movement, when the final eight bars repeat the first eight (albeit transposed, reversed and rhythmically altered), does the derivation begin to become apparent.

By comparison with this elaborate structure, the brief third movement is almost naïve in its playfulness: the four 'scherzo' sections are recognizably related (they may readily be analysed as statement, retrograde inversion, restatement, and retrograde), the three 'trios' a little less so. The fourth movement, however, is again as ramified a construction as the first. Beginning with three and a half pages of desperate suggestions around the basic ideas, it plunges into the bass for an ominous serial statement which gives rise to the first quasi-fugue. This settles into a soft 'grisaille sonore', but that is not maintained for long before Boulez hurls out motifs 'dans une nuance forte, exaspérée'. Another, longer contrapuntal development leads to a climax of expressive vehemence, where the piano truly must be 'remarkably prone to frenzy' as it deals with such markings as 'encore plus violent' and 'pulveriser le son'. The final page, however, is one of tranquillity in which motifs from throughout the sonata are gently nudged to mind.

The violence of the first and last movements of the Second Sonata is not just superficial: it is expressive of a whole aesthetic of annihilation, and in particular of a need to obliterate what had gone before. As Boulez has said: 'History as it is made by great composers is not a history of conservation but of destruction—even while cherishing what is being destroyed.' The highly charged developments of the Second Sonata bring an auto-destructive impetus to the classical moulds of sonata allegro and fugue, a determined refutation of Schoenberg's conservative practice with regard to form. At the same time, Boulez's techniques of rhythmic manipulation rapidly destroy the profiles of his cells, and his proliferating serial method threatens the unifying power of the series. One need look no further than Ex. 1, from *Le Visage nuptial*, for confirmation that this last destruction proceeded through love.

The all-consuming power of love is the poetic centre of this, Boulez's first vocal work. René Char's five poems speak in hard-edged surrealist imagery of an ecstatic sexual passion, and Boulez took their invitation to range rapidly through emotional territory on the borders of fevered hysteria. The richness and density of his expression would seem to demand big resources, yet the work was originally scored for a small ensemble of soprano, contralto, two ondes martenot, piano, and percussion. Only in 1951–2 was it revised with the addition of a women's chorus and the replacement of the instrumental quartet by a large orchestra.

In this version *Le Visage nuptial* has a hectically varied orchestral colouring, bounding far beyond its sources in Berg and Messiaen, though the string writing, often in many parts so that chords can be spread and decorated, is quite original. So too is the precision with which Boulez uses modes of articulation between song and speech (he adds one to those employed by Berg), and the finesse of his quarter-tone writing, which may have been stimulated by the presence in Paris of the Russian quarter-tone pioneer Ivan Vishnegradsky. *Le Visage nuptial* has a more outspoken, because identified, passion than any other of Boulez's early works, but its extraordinary demands have militated against frequent performance.

Boulez's other René Char cantata of this period, *Le Soleil des eaux*, has a complex history of performance and revision. In 1948 Boulez wrote music for a radio production of Char's play of the same name, this score apparently including settings of two poems, 'Complainte du lézard amoureux' and 'La Sorgue', specially written for the broadcast version. These were adapted to form a brief concert work for soprano, tenor, bass, and orchestra, which was performed in 1950. The piece was revised with added choral parts in 1958, and in 1965 it became a work for soprano, chorus, and orchestra. According to Boulez's own account, the changes were concerned with achieving a good balance between voices and instruments, particularly in 'La Sorgue', but comparison of the two published versions (those of 1958 and 1965) shows also how the orchestration has become more sophisticated. This is apparent right from the opening, as is demonstrated in Ex. 10. Webernian timbre-melody has been converted into something much more Boulezian, with a characteristic 'rounding up' of melodic notes in chords:

Ex. 10

It is not only in details of orchestration that the versions of the first movement, 'Complainte du lézard amoureux', differ: the solo soprano line, which had required varied tendencies towards speech in the 1958 version, becomes pure song in the 1965 revision. For the most part this vocal line is interleaved with orchestral episodes which serve as musical and poetic commentaries. The poem is a love song addressed by a lizard to a goldfinch flying above him in the heat of a summer day in Char's native Provence, and the setting is appropriately fresh and lyrical, the word-painting unusually direct for Boulez, as when the bird is advised to seek refuge in the meadow grass and the orchestra offers a dense, weaving superimposition of canons.

The solo soprano, whose monody is essentially palindromic, begins by taking up the series announced in Ex. 10:

Ex. 11

but, like the orchestra, she soon departs from serial orthodoxy in an improvisatory flight which touches on all kinds of suggestion without ever coming to ground. Many of the rhythmic cells are, as here, in even values, but the basic unit is always in flux, so that one has only a fleeting impression of pulse. Similarly, there is a supple play on tonal references. The section 'Chardonneret . . . reviens', for instance, has the notes of an E♭ triad giving place to a whole-tone configuration and then, at what is a return of the Sonatina's 'x' motif, a suggestion of Messiaenic modality. So the song proceeds.

'La Sorgue', a kind of ecological protest, is utterly different. In Char's play the river Sorgue is the source of livelihood for a community who have fished it for generations, and who find themselves threatened by pollution from a factory on its banks. The poem is an apostrophe to the river, acknowledging its strength and independence, but demanding its assistance, and Boulez's setting gives full weight to the imprecation with shouting chorus and a bounding quaver rhythm, dissolving (in the definitive version) into a soprano melisma with flowing orchestral accompaniment.

Le Soleil des eaux and the Second Sonata mark the end of a period in which Boulez, still only twenty-three, had proved he could master and bring together everything he chose to learn from his predecessors. Often—and most obviously in the Second Sonata, 'La Sorgue', and *Le Visage nuptial*—the result is music of emotional tempest: the music of a young man impatient with anything less than total engagement in advancing creative thought, and also that of one who had been 'struck in a very violent way' by the beauty of African and far eastern music, 'a beauty so far removed from our own culture and so close to my own temperament'. He had found, moreover, a poetic model nearer home, as he acknowledged at the end of his first technical essay, 'Propositions' (1948), in a rare moment of openness about his expressive aims. 'I think', he wrote, 'that music must be hysteria and collective spells, violently of the present—following the direction of Antonin Artaud . . . but I have a horror of treating verbally what people complacently call aesthetic problems . . . I prefer to return to my ruled paper.'

'AT THE ENDS OF FRUITFUL LAND . . .'

THE work that Boulez returned to his ruled paper to write was his *Livre pour quatuor* for string quartet (1948–9), his first instrumental work without piano. The new medium imposed, as Boulez has said, 'a certain reticence', but it also made available a wider variety of tone colour, for he was able to pursue all the effects of articulation and texture to be found in the quartets of Debussy, Bartók, Berg, and Webern, particularly Webern's Op. 5 and Op. 9. Yet the sensuous abstraction of the *Livre* is more than a matter of delicate interplays of timbre: it depends also on the judicious balance of severity with improvisatory fantasy. Movements II and VI (and perhaps also IV, which has not been published or performed) are those in which attention is drawn most closely to the development of motifs in an intensive manner proceeding from the Second Piano Sonata. The odd-numbered pieces (Ia, Ib, IIIa, IIIb, IIIc, and V) are, by contrast, freer in feeling and motion. Ia and Ib, for example, combine to make an ambling variation which leads back to the note from which it started out, with vague melodic strands to set the music moving again whenever it comes to a halt in a trilling chord.

However, the opposition between the two kinds of movement is not absolute. There are passages in the even-numbered ones which have as much pure appeal as the others, such as the section of swooping high-altitude harmonics in II, and sometimes the fine-woven decoration of the odd-numbered movements is stripped to motivic essentials. This happens most dramatically in IIIb, where the characteristic texture, of melodic figures playing on planes of sustained tones, is abruptly torn apart at the end. Moreover, all the movements have the kind of form in which ideas are made to proliferate, whether in hard-pressed argument (II), free variation with veiled suggestion of return (Ia), or continuous succession (IIIc). There are now no structural schemes to destroy; instead each movement seems to consider its material with speculative detachment.

This feeling of detachment is strengthened by the layout of the music, the use of the quartet more as a single sounding-body than as an ensemble of individuals. The crossings of parts, the scarcity of long lines and the rapid changes of timbre all serve to confuse the separate voices and, in performance, to remove one's awareness of four musicians physically playing. This, and the technical difficulty of the *Livre*, denies the individual performer an 'interpretative' role, just as he is dissuaded from that role in the Second Sonata by Boulez's injunction to 'avoid absolutely, above all in slow tempos, what are commonly known as "expressive nuances"'. Boulez is not of course insisting that the music be inexpressive, merely that expression is a matter for the composer, whether it be the frenzied vehemence of the sonata or the shifting nervosity of the *Livre*.

If the *Livre* marks an expressive movement inwards, it also shows a further stage in Boulez's attempt to form a coherent compositional technique which might bring rhythm and timbre into rapport with the serialism of pitch: hence, in particular, the ramified working of rhythmic cells in the even-numbered movements. The rhythmic complexity of the *Livre* places it at the limits of any quartet's capability, which accounts for its delayed and piecemeal first performance: movements I and II were first heard in 1955, V and VI in 1961, and III in 1962. Partial performances are, however, not in contradiction with the nature of the work, for the players are invited to choose and order movements as they will, though there is some doubt as to whether this aleatory freedom was part of the original conception.

By the late sixties Boulez had decided that the *Livre* could not be played adequately without a conductor, and so he withdrew it (except for performances by quartets who had already learned it) and set about a new version for large string orchestra, *Livre pour cordes*. But, characteristically, he could not be content with a simple transcription. The new work, of which only sections Ia and Ib have been completed, is an elaborate amplification which spreads in varying densities around the original, giving it veils of fine counterpoint and harmonic breadth.

Meanwhile Boulez had returned to the pressing problem of the moment, which was the establishment of an integrated serial technique along the lines suggested to him as he worked on the sixth movement of the *Livre pour quatuor*. Progress was not immediate: there was a gap of two years before, in 1951–2, he made various approaches to 'total serialism' in the first book of *Structures* for two pianos, *Polyphonie X* for eighteen instruments, and the two *Études* on magnetic tape. Though they are not named, these are the works surveyed in his article 'Eventuellement . . .' (1952), a theoretical and polemical document which begins with a defensive justification of his rigorous exploration of compositional fundamentals. 'What then remains for us to attempt', he asks, 'if not to gather together the bundle of possibilities elaborated by our predecessors, while exacting from it a minimum of constructive logic? At a time of transformation and organization, when the problem of language imposes itself with a particular acuity and so, it seems, musical *grammar* declines for a while, we take up our responsibilities, with intransigence.'

As in the works of 1946–8, Boulez was seeing it as his duty to combine the advances of the Second Viennese School with those of Stravinsky and Messiaen, but now in a clear, precise manner which could be justified logically. The first task was to find a unified technique for handling the basic constituents of music—pitch, duration, loudness, and timbre—and Boulez found an essay towards this in Messiaen's 'Mode de valeurs et d'intensités' for piano (1949), which uses 'modes' of twelve chromatic pitches, twelve durations, seven intensities, and twelve methods of attack. Messiaen had here opened the possibility of a generalized serial technique in which all the basic musical elements might be handled according to the same rules, and Boulez followed this up in section Ia from *Structures*, the *locus classicus* of total serialism.

The series for *Structures* (Ex. 12 shows its initial statement in the first piano):

Ex. 12

is derived from the first mode in Messiaen's 'Mode de valeurs'. From it the composition of *Structures Ia* proceeds in large part automatically through the construction of a number square. Boulez numbers the pitches of the series from 1 to 12 (E = 1, D = 2, A = 3, etc.) and uses the same numbering for every transposition, so that, for example, the transposition by a diminished seventh, D–C–G–etc., is numbered 2–8–4–etc. The resulting number sequences are then arranged vertically following the order in the original series (i.e. with the sequence beginning with 1 on top, then the sequence beginning with 2, and so on) to produce a twelve-by-twelve square of numbers. The inversion of the series, together with its transpositions, will generate a second square; the retrograde and retrograde inversion forms can be obtained from these two squares simply by reading from right to left.

As Ligeti has shown in his comprehensive analysis of *Structures Ia*, Boulez uses the number squares as sources of series for dynamic levels and attacks, by reading diagonally and interpreting the numbers as specific qualities (1 as *pppp* and 12 as *ffff*, for example, in a series of dynamics). Duration series are obtained from horizontal sequences by converting the figures into numbers of demisemiquavers: Ex. 12 shows one such. Boulez then simply lays out all forty-eight forms of the pitch series, each with a particular duration series and some with serial dynamics and attacks as well, in fourteen sections of varying density, from one to six statements being overlain. The details of the serial technique, which are very easy to analyse, need not be considered further here. More interesting are the secondary decisions which Boulez takes after the serial framework has, as it were, invented itself.

These secondary decisions involve register, tempo, and density, and Ex. 13 gives some indication of how these aspects are varied in *Structures Ia* so that Boulez achieves variety and symmetry in what might have been a piece of undifferentiated stasis:

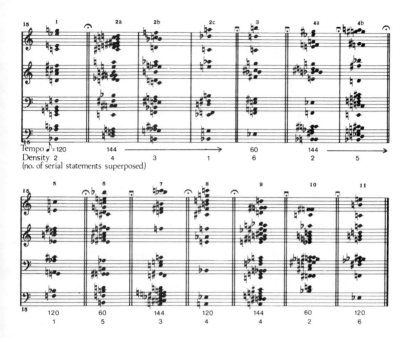

One may note, for example, the palindromic arrangements of tempos, the increasing and increasingly stable density, the preponderance of the bass register in section 7, the upper in 8, and the middle in 9 and 10, and the changing degree to which notes are fixed in register, this being total in sections 2c, 3, 5, and 8 (inevitably so, of course, in the single-strand sections 2c and 5), and nearly total in 11 (one 'roving' pitch). The fixing of register is especially interesting, for it is a technique which Boulez had used in the Second Sonata, though to very different effect. There the prominence of particular notes had given a sense of desperate insistence, whereas in *Structures Ia* the impression is of something more abstract, of what Ligeti has aptly called 'knots' in the serial web. The effect is of course most pronounced in sections of high density, such as 2a (see Ex. 14), where the increasingly forceful presence of an E♭ provides a point of focus and a remnant of order.

Modéré, presque vif (♪=144)

So it is that the secondary decisions give shape to *Structures Ia*, that shape being imposed on a serial structure much more obvious to the analyst's eye than the listener's ear. The serial statements are generally so interwoven that they cannot be distinguished, and the serialism of elements other than pitch goes quite unrecognized, except inasmuch as the duration serialism brings about a direct relation between density and rhythmic regularity (clearly, when several statements of the duration series are superposed there is a tendency to even demisemiquaver pulsation). But the attempt at total serialism had had to be made, and it was made in the full knowledge that it represented an abstention from creative decision-making. Boulez had sought this way not only to combine the innovations of his predecessors but also to eliminate their influence—not, as before, through destruction, but by making any influence impossible. *Structures Ia* was an exploration, to quote the Klee title originally intended for it, 'at the ends of fruitful land . . .'.

The work that followed was *Polyphonie X*, written in the same year of 1951 and scored for an ensemble of eleven wind instruments and seven strings, all treated as soloists. Its title indicates not that it was the tenth work in a series, but that it was an essay in that 'cross polyphony', that diagonal thinking, which had captured Boulez's imagination from the beginning. He had seen Webern's abolition of the boundary between harmonic and melodic compo-sition, particularly in the Second Cantata, as opening this new diagonal perspective, which often seems in his music to mean a sophisticated form of retrograde canon (the next chapter will provide an example). Beyond that, *Polyphonie X* was again an exercise in total serial control, though of a different kind from that in *Structures Ia*.

The rhythmic organization does not use arithmetical duration series but rather quasi-serial manipulations of cells: there are seven basic cells and seven ways of altering them. The instrumentation, too, is ordered along serial lines, the ensemble being divided at any time into, again, seven groups. To judge from accounts of the only performance and a few published extracts, all this required a neglect of instrumentalists' capacities and of sonorous appeal, and the work has long been withdrawn for revision.

Moving forward from what he has described as the 'theoretical exaggeration' of *Polyphonie X*, Boulez began to loosen the rigours of *Structures Ia* in composing the third and last of the pieces which make up this first book. One may guess that he had been most dissatisfied with the rhythmic automatism of the first piece, for the liveliness of *Structures Ic* depends largely on the introduction of new rhythmic techniques. Again the music consists entirely of complete linear statements of the pitch series, but these no longer occur in regular segments. The first of the three sections mixes arithmetical duration series with sequences of even values:

Ex. 15

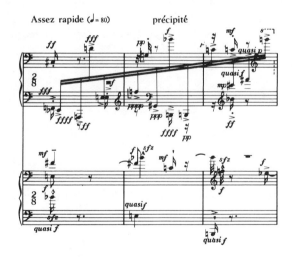

Here one statement of the duration series, in the right hand of the second piano, is combined with sequences in regular semiquavers, dotted quavers, crotchets, crotchets plus demisemiquavers, and dotted crotchets. As a result the density shifts more freely than in *Structures Ia*, and the form can be articulated by rapid regular successions at the beginning, midpoint, and end. The second and third sections add further diversity in sequences obtained by diagonal readings of the number squares, these predominating in the third section. They cannot be heard for what they are, but they do bring about a suppleness in the rhythmic texture, with bursts of short values appearing unpredictably, and the new techniques also make possible a rhythmic loosening in the piece, from the weighting of regular sequences in the first section to the irregular flow of the third.

Structures Ib, the last piece of the set to be composed, is much the longest and most complex. It is also a piece of much greater significance in Boulez's output than the exceptional *Structures Ia*. Boulez would appear to have decided that the moderate liberation of *Ic* was insufficient, that he needed to go back to his old free handling of intervallic and rhythmic units, and perhaps that, after the strict discipline of the other pieces, he could now do so without fear of plagiarizing others. But, transfigured by the experience of compositional rigour, the turbulent variety of the earlier works now has the more abstract aspect of creative virtuosity.

It is no longer possible in *Structures Ib* to follow Boulez's serial workings in detail, even though the notation invites the application of the analyst's wits. Ex. 16, for instance, shows a curious bar from early in the second piano part:

Ex. 16

Clearly this notation has no meaning for performer or listener, but it does turn out to be necessary to the deduction of the rhythmic structure at this point, and the piece is also full of vertical lines to mark off serial fragments. This may be 'Augenmusik', but one should remember that Boulez was attempting to lay the foundations of a new musical grammar: those foundations had to be exposed if they were to be of any use to future builders.

Boulez returns here to his use of the series to generate a 'certain texture of intervals', with the minor second and its various octave transpositions given pride of place. He returns also to his earlier flexibility of motion, re-introducing irrational values and grace notes, and, as in the slow movement of the Second Sonata, interpolating pauses: a passage such as that shown in Ex. 17 is well on the way to the supple movement of *Le Marteau sans maître*:

Ex. 17

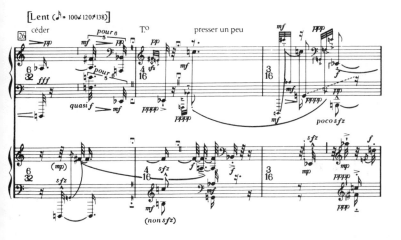

Formally, too, *Structures Ib* takes up the more characteristic method of balancing different kinds of motion, though the structure is still quite clearly symmetrical. Sections in strict fast tempo are alternated with passages allowing mobility within a given slow tempo range, the former being short two-part counterpoints, the latter more complicated and longer. The contrasts of tempo are extreme, but there is a disparity between written tempo and experienced tempo because the predominant note values also change widely. The opening 'Très rapide', for instance, sounds slower than the 'Lent' which follows it, for the prevailing crotchet, minim, and semibreve durations of the former are replaced by demisemiquavers. Such ambiguities, which are not without effect in a good performance, were again to be taken up in later works.

Structures Ib came at the end of a period of intensive 'research', during which Boulez had found himself obliged to produce the unpleasant *Polyphonie X* and the *Études* which forswear all the evocative resonances of *musique concrète*, concentrating instead on serial cuttings of neutral material. With the new piece he had come through that particular tunnel, and even if his earlier expressive power had not yet been recaptured, at least more fruitful lands were in sight.

LE MARTEAU SANS MAÎTRE

IN 1953, the year after the completion of *Structures I*, Boulez began work on his first full-scale composition with the techniques he had developed beyond total serialism. He may have intended the new work as a demonstration that he could now approach again the expressive territory of his first works, for he turned, as he had in 1946, to the poetry of René Char. However, the three poems he chose came from an earlier collection, *Le Marteau sans maître*, from which his piece took its title. The verse is very much more concise, its stark, obscure images hammered into a few lines, and the tone is less directly personal. In both respects the poems suited Boulez's aim, which was not so much to set them to music as to use them as the essence of elaborate musical forms.

Only four of the nine movements of *Le Marteau* are vocal, and only one, the third, could be considered a 'song'. In the others the poem is not the music's master but its generating seed, and this relationship is continued in the instrumental movements. Each poem gives rise to a little cycle of musical glosses: 'L'Artisanat furieux', sung in movement III, has a prelude (I) and a postlude (VII); 'Bourreaux de solitude' (VI) has three commentaries (II, IV, VIII); and 'Bel Édifice et les pressentiments' (V) has a 'double', or variation (IX). As will be seen, the three cycles are interwoven, but each has distinctive features of rhythm, texture, instrumentation, and vocal style.

It is on its instrumentation that the qualities of *Le Marteau* depend to an unusual degree, even though Boulez's ensemble has been endlessly imitated. The work is scored for contralto voice, alto flute, viola, guitar, vibraphone, xylorimba, and unpitched percussion instruments (one player), a grouping whose reference to that of *Pierrot lunaire* is pointed in the voice/flute duo of the third movement. However, the weighting of percussion instruments suggests more exotic models: according to Boulez, the vibraphone relates to the Balinese gamelan, the xylorimba to the music of black Africa, and the guitar (a more dubious connection) to the sound of the Japanese koto. One of the marvels of *Le Marteau* is that these alien references are not only clear but also integrated, more completely so than in earlier works by Messiaen and Boulez himself (*Le Visage nuptial*).

There was another, equally important consideration governing

Boulez's choice of instruments for *Le Marteau*, and that was his wish to make the ensemble at once varied and unified. The alto range is overstepped only by the guitar and the xylorimba, both of which produce the most evanescent sensation of pitch. Moreover, as Boulez has explained, the voice connects with the alto flute as an instrument of breath, the alto flute with the viola as a sustaining instrument, the viola (pizzicato) with the guitar as a plucked string instrument, the guitar with the vibraphone as a resonator, and the vibraphone with the xylorimba as an instrument to be struck. The percussion he leaves out of account as 'marginal', though the xylorimba's high noise content establishes some connection.

As is clear from Ex. 18, the instrumental correspondences are used in the composition, in that related groupings are normally chosen:

Ex. 18

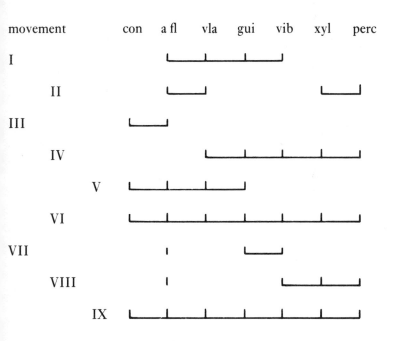

The main exception is in the increasingly isolated position accorded the alto flute in movements VII and VIII, and this is not without significance, as will appear. One may also note from Ex. 18 that certain features of instrumentation are used to characterize the cycles. That on 'Bourreaux de solitude' (II, IV, VI, VIII), for instance, is marked by the constant presence of the xylorimba and the percussion, which are absent from all other movements but the last. By contrast, the 'L'Artisanat furieux' (I, III, VII) cycle emphasizes the sustaining-monodic part of the spectrum.

The vocal movement of this cycle is the voice/flute duo. Ex. 19 shows the setting of the poem's first line, which is representative of the ornate vocal style and the tangential relation between voice and alto flute in this piece:

Ex. 19

The opening flute solo, beginning with a typical Boulezian flourish, has little in common with the vocal entry which follows, but then the flute announces a twelve-note series which is an almost exact retrograde inversion of the contralto's on 'du clou'. Other moments of imitation occur sporadically, and at the end of the movement the two lines nestle into each other in another serial statement:

Ex. 20

Both the prelude and the postlude to 'L'Artisanat furieux' take place at double speed: they are, as it were, 'harmonics' of the song. Both allude to the vocal movement also in their counterpointing of two parts which now and then close together. Ex. 21 shows the first section of 'Avant "L'Artisanat furieux"', a passage which Boulez's solid rectangles invite one to analyse:

Ex. 21

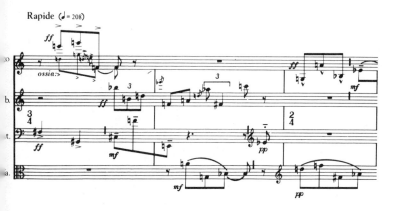

It is clear that the music is in two parts, flute and vibraphone being set against guitar and viola, and that each part has five segments (the case is rarely so straightforward). These segments relate to one another diagonally, so that the section can be considered an example of that 'cross polyphony' previously mentioned. Not only that, the five segments refer more or less obliquely to the first five words of the setting (see Ex. 19): the alto flute's final G♯–F♯ in Ex. 21 both parallels the E–D at 'bord' and is presaged by the guitar's initial F♯–G♯. A few moments' examination of Exx. 19 and 21 will reveal other correspondences, of both rhythmic cell and intervallic motif.

The first commentary on 'Bourreaux de solitude', which follows 'Avant "L'Artisanat furieux"', presents a bald contrast. Fast fluid polyphony is replaced by a heterophonic working out of rhythmic cells in strict tempo, melodic play by percussive insistence, the viola being played pizzicato throughout. Furthermore, the continuous, though interrupted, activity of the first movement gives way to a clear ternary form, the middle section marked by a faster tempo, the loss of the alto flute, and a change of percussion instrument. In the longer term, however, it is the 'L'Artisanat furieux' cycle which impresses itself as a ternary structure, with the vocal movement placed between two comparable instrumental pieces, while the 'Bourreaux de solitude' cycle has a more homogeneous character.

This character springs from the poem, whose imagery of time is interpreted in the cellular rhythmic developments of the three commentaries, all of them somewhat Balinese in effect. It is perhaps the hours and the minutes that are the 'hangmen of solitude': time weighs heavy, and in the second commentary it falls every so often to a standstill, the pulsed movement being frozen to leave a resonating note or chord:

Ex. 22

When it comes to the vocal movement, the pulse has almost disappeared, leaving only fugitive suggestions in the pianissimo maracas part. The texture is now one of labouring harmonic skeins, into which the voice is woven for a syllabic statement of the poem in disjunct lines. Finally, the third commentary repeats the 'killing of time' in miniature, and the virtuoso alto flute part seems to make sense of earlier melodic material (for flute in the first commentary and for viola in the latter part of the second) by alluding to the voice of the poetic setting.

'Bel Édifice et les pressentiments', in its first version, stands as an intermediary between the settings of the other poems, for the vocal line is melismatic yet not so highly decorated as that of 'L'Artisanat furieux'. With regard to the integration of voice and instrument(s), it is again at a midpoint between the voice-centred 'L'Artisanat' and the ensemble-centred 'Bourreaux', the contralto being set in a texture of trills and brilliant figuration. This is in some ways the most relaxed movement, and illustration of the text is here most direct. Ex. 23 shows, for instance, how the word 'promenade' is interpreted in ambling instrumental homophony and 'sauvage' in a fierce vocal gesture:

Ex. 23

The second setting of 'Bel Édifice', nominally a 'double' of the first, in fact begins (Ex. 24a) by recalling a moment from 'Bourreaux de solitude' (Ex. 24b), the link, of course, being in the text. Another verbal relation later provides the occasion for a memory of 'L'Artisanat furieux', with voice and guitar (Ex. 25a) partly redistributing the original lines for voice and alto flute (25b).

However, much of the piece is indeed a variation of the first 'Bel Édifice', though the voice is usually stifled into abrupt Sprechgesang,

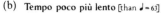

as in Ex. 24a. The introduction of elements from the other vocal movements, in the tempos of those movements, is simply a preparation for the combination which takes place in the larger part of the movement (bars 42–188) when the vocal setting is over.

Ex. 25

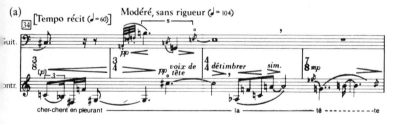

Much of this consists of music for xylorimba, vibraphone, guitar, viola, and humming voice, music which switches in tempo and style between the first setting of 'Bel Édifice' and that of 'Bourreaux de solitude'. The remaining vocal movement, 'L'Artisanat furieux', is present in several interruptions for alto flute and percussion (gong and tam tams). Ex. 26 shows the opening of the last of these, in which the beginning of 'L'Artisanat furieux' (Ex. 19) reappears in oblique, shattered fashion: compare, for example, the fourth bar of Ex. 26 with the setting of 'rouge' and 'La':

Ex. 26

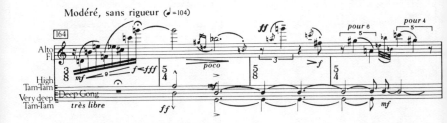

Moreover, it has become clear, within this final movement, that the flute has taken over from the voice, a development foreshadowed at the end of 'L'Artisanat furieux' (Ex. 20) and also within the 'Bourreaux de solitude' cycle, and prepared by the increasing isolation of the flute in movements VII and VIII. Music has usurped the place of words, as it does throughout *Le Marteau*, and the work ends with music itself displaced as the flute's last tone dissolves into the resonance of a large suspended cymbal.

Only in this respect does *Le Marteau* display any straight line of development. Its processes are generally circuitous and allusive, as the examples given here will have indicated. The links which have been described between the first three vocal movements and the finale are relations of suggestion rather than statement, and so it is in the small-scale progress of the music. Ex. 21, for instance, is less likely to be heard as a piece of two-part reversible counterpoint than as a rapid succession of vaguely related images, as music whose constant change is laced with fleeting echoes. Rapidity of change, which is not always a function of tempo, is indeed an important variable in *Le Marteau*, and it is in terms of this feature, as well as the cross-references and underlying intervallic constancies (the major second and, still more so, the minor third are important base units), that the work is best understood.

Certainly it resists any kind of conventional serial analysis, despite the presence of twelve-note statements as in Exx. 19 and 20. By now Boulez had come to an understanding of the series which had been implicit in his earliest published works and only briefly abandoned in his speculative investigation of total serialism. 'The series is not an order of succession', he wrote in his article '" . . . Auprès et au loin"' (1954), 'but indeed a hierarchy—which may be independent of this order of succession.' This means that the series can, by means which Boulez puts forward in his treatise *Penser la musique aujourd'hui* (1963), give rise to a vast range of possibilities having some more or less close connection with an initial idea, perhaps a small intervallic motif.

In '" . . . Auprès et au loin"' Boulez also distinguishes between 'rigorous style' and 'free style', two poles which may be represented in *Le Marteau* by 'Commentaire I de "Bourreaux de solitude"' and 'L'Artisanat furieux'. However, one is not to suppose that the 'free style' is the result of free composition. In *Penser la musique aujourd'hui* Boulez quotes a fragment from the alto flute part in 'Commentaire III de "Bourreaux de solitude"':

Ex. 27

and notes that its freedom is carefully contrived: 'Starting from an extreme rigidity of conception—of practically canonic writing—a suppleness of realization is reached which can easily be mistaken for a flexible improvisation.' 'More and more', as he wrote four years later, 'I find that in order to create effectively one has to consider delirium and, yes, organize it.'

Le Marteau sans maître does indeed owe its effect to the completeness with which the delirium of a violent surrealism is considered and organized, to a rational technique's straining to encompass the extremes of the irrational. Its importance lies also in Boulez's discovery, through his proliferating serial method, of the means to create music which neither apes the quasi-narrative forms of tonality nor contents itself with simple symmetries in the manner of *Structures*. This was the discovery that Boulez celebrated at the close of his dictionary definition of 'series': 'Classical tonal thought', he wrote, 'is based on a universe defined by gravitation and attraction; serial thought on a universe in perpetual expansion.'

'ALÉA'

THE next step was to make 'perpetual expansion' a real presence by creating works which might change, in detail and in form, from one performance to another. This Boulez undertook in three compositions begun in 1956–7: the Third Piano Sonata, the second book of *Structures* for two pianos and *Pli selon pli* for soprano and orchestra. The development may well have been stimulated by the 'chance composition' of Cage, whom Boulez had met in 1949 and whose prepared piano he had hailed as an important contribution. By this time, however, he had distanced himself far from Cage's ideas, and his article 'Aléa' (1957), in which he set the conditions for his own aleatory composition, attacks Cage without naming him: 'the individual does not feel responsible for his work, but merely throws himself by unadmitted weakness, by confusion, and for temporary assuagement into puerile magic.' 'Aléa' is equally critical of those for whom 'schematization, quite simply, takes the place of invention' (the danger of *Structures Ia*) to produce what Boulez dismisses as 'slices of chance', and of those who would leave a wide degree of freedom to the performer. For him the need is not to introduce chance but to limit its field of action, and that need has been made urgent by his own experience. 'Despairingly', he writes, 'one tries to dominate one's material by an arduous, sustained, vigilant effort, and despairingly chance persists, slips in through a thousand unstoppable loopholes. "And it's fine that way!" Nevertheless, wouldn't the composer's ultimate ruse be to *absorb* this chance?'

Chance is to be absorbed, Boulez goes on to suggest, in musical structures which depend on a degree of latitude, perhaps in tempo: this he had already done in *Structure Ib* and *Le Marteau sans maître*. Chance can also be accommodated in musical forms which are inherently mobile, and this possibility he explored most fully in the Third Piano Sonata. There are five movements, or 'formants', which can be arranged in eight different ways, each formant containing its own smaller formal mobilities. All this is sketched out in Boulez's article '"Sonata, que me veux-tu?"', in which he also mentions the possibility of 'developpants', other movements which would be 'strikingly distinct but nonetheless related by their structure to the initial formants'. However, so far from growing in this way, the sonata has remained a torso, with only two complete formants, *Trope* and *Constellation-Miroir*, in print.

Trope provides a clear example of how a mobile form can develop as the necessary outcome of principles present within the series. Indeed, Boulez may have set out in the Third Sonata to demonstrate that the serial method, which is permutational, logically entails permutable forms, for serial derivations are here much more obvious than in any other of his works except the outer pieces of *Structures I*. In the case of *Trope*, the series is considered as a succession of four units, and this partitioning suggests cyclical concatenations of serial forms (see Ex. 28). Furthermore, two of the serial units, *b* and *d*, together contain the pitches of *a* transposed down a minor third: the foreign group *c*, itself symmetrical, is a 'trope' which interrupts the larger symmetry.

These features of the series are mirrored in the formant, which also has four subsections, 'Texte', 'Parenthèse', 'Commentaire', and 'Glose', these being, so one may deduce, projections of the groups *a*, *b*, *c*, and *d*. 'Glose' and 'Commentaire' can be exchanged in position, so, as it were, making manifest the symmetry within the series. The player can also begin with any one of the sections and proceed cyclically through the rest (the formant is spirally bound to facilitate this), just as the series opens itself to cyclical permutation. However, it makes most sense to begin with the simplest section, as Charles Rosen does in the recording made under Boulez's supervision, adopting the order T–P–G–C.

Apart from following its series in structure, *Trope* also, as the title suggests, takes up the idea of 'troping', to the extent that the music abounds in interpolated or superimposed commentaries on its development. Boulez had used this technique in the slow movement of the Second Piano Sonata and in *Structures Ib*, but here there are parenthetic comments which do not have to be played (though in Rosen's recording they all are). Ex. 29, from the opening of 'Parenthèse', shows one of these 'footnotes' introduced into a simple serial structure, that of Ex. 28. It is not difficult to see how, in terms of serial groupings, this forms a comment on what has been played and a lead-back to the next obligatory passage. In terms of what is heard, the most important features are the contrast of strict with free tempo and

Ex. 28

original series

original series + diminished fifth

retrograde inversion

retrograde inversion + diminished fifth

Ex. 29

Nettement au dessous de Lent (♩=40)

the sense of 'correction' when the second obligatory passage repeats an E–F fall in the free material.

If *Trope* is thus effective as, to use Boulez's words, 'the object of its own reflection', it impresses itself less successfully as a cyclical form. Instead it appears to develop in strophes, particularly when played in the order which Rosen adopts. 'Texte', a moderately complex fixed piece, is 'explained' in the simple fixed structure of 'Parenthèse' and elaborated in its free commentaries. 'Glose', also fixed, then disguises the text with clusters, and 'Commentaire' brings it to fullest development in both obligatory and optional passages. Moreover, the ending of 'Commentaire', with deep fortissimo trills followed by sforzato chords over the whole keyboard, comes as a properly final dismissal.

Constellation-Miroir, a retrograde version of the unpublished *Constellation*, is a more palpably open form and a more complex one. The music is laid out on several large sheets in six 'constellations' of material, three of 'Points' (single-note structures) printed in green, two of 'Blocs' (massive chords and arpeggios) printed in red, and a brief 'Mélange' of both. These must be played in the order 'Mélange'—'Points 3'—'Blocs II'—'Points 2'—'Blocs I'—'Points I', but within each section the player may choose from several possible arrangements of the fragments. Boulez has likened the piece to a map of an unknown city, around which the performer 'must direct himself through a tight network of routes'. Unforeseen, subtle connections infiltrate the paths, and these give the formant its feeling of labyrinthine openness. Hardly less impressive is the fluidity of movement or the diversity of sounds achieved from different pedallings and the resonances of undamped strings, so that the music has a tonal appeal to match the visual distinction of the score.

The 'Blocs' of *Constellation-Miroir* make abundant use of the technique of 'chord multiplication' which Boulez described in his 1952 article 'Eventuellement . . .', and which is one of his most powerful contributions to serial thought. Ex. 30, an extract from 'Blocs I', shows the technique in operation. Its last chord, for example, can be obtained by 'squaring' a chord derived from that series (it is an instance of the *a* of *Trope*), as in Ex. 31. The first chord in this example is transposed on to every degree of the second, and so one obtains an eight-note chord which, with register changes, gives rise to the final chord of Ex. 30; note too that the parent chord provides the preceding right-hand arpeggio. In this way Boulez is able to compose chains of related harmonies, and in this case, as in the 'Blocs' generally, the

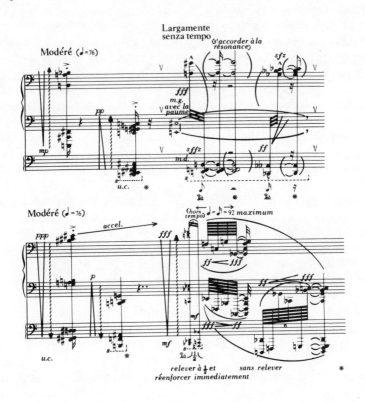

Ex. 31

relation is emphasized by the restricted range, each structure
suggesting a locking into a specific harmonic field.

If mobile form seems an almost inevitable consequence of Boulez's
wide-ranging serial technique at this stage, it is impossible to ignore
the literary parallels which pointed his way. The layout of
Constellation-Miroir evokes the memory of Mallarmé's *Un Coup de*

dès, which similarly has lines straddling across the pages to admit a multiplicity of different readings, and the Third Sonata as a whole can be seen as a musical reflection on Mallarmé's projected *Livre*, which was to have been a mobile instrument of words, leaves, and volumes.

Boulez was also impressed by the work of Joyce, whose verbal ambiguities are widely imitated in the Third Sonata: in Ex. 28, for instance, the connecting units act as musical puns, to be understood in two senses at the same time (though this technique also derives from Webern's serial practice). Joyce's stylistic plurality, the other feature of his technique which interested Boulez, is most notably emulated in the second book of *Structures* for two pianos (1956–61), in connection with which Boulez asked: 'Does a musical work have to be considered as a formal construction with a firmly fixed direction? Could one not try to regard it as a fantastic succession, in which the "stories" have no rigid relationship, no fixed order?'

Structures II is divided into two 'chapters', of which the first does have a fixed order. Here Boulez uses chord multiplication more cogently than in *Constellation-Miroir*, establishing harmonic fields into which the two pianos summon each other:

Ex. 32

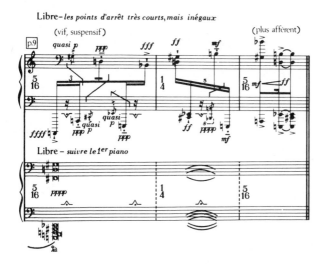

or which they superpose. The succession of fields, though 'fantastic', can be felt to lead more or less directly to the ending, where both pianists alight on the same B♭, this prepared by the use of harmonies symmetrically disposed around that note. Equally essential to the sense of wayward directedness is Boulez's finesse in composing with different kinds of musical motion to produce a fluid inter-cutting of speeds.

The second chapter is more varied in style, this variety being necessary to the articulation of a mobile form in which Boulez uses the new possibilities available with a duo. Not only does each part contain elements which can be differently arranged, but the players are required to give manual signals to each other at various points. Ex. 33 shows both kinds of mobility, with, at the end of the example, the second pianist giving the first an indication that he may begin his 'Première pièce', which is one of several 'stories' with no rigid relationship to its context:

Ex. 33

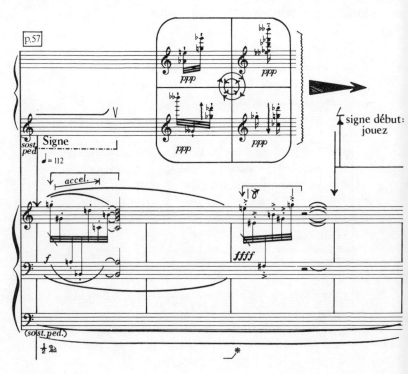

A toccata-like cadenza in the extreme treble, this 'Première pièce' stands out boldly from the flexible continuity of the second chapter, though not all the inserts are placed so much in relief.

Boulez's allegiance to the aesthetics of Mallarmé, implicit in *Structures II* as well as the Third Sonata, becomes fully stated in *Pli selon pli* (1957–62), which is a 'portrait' of the poet, a disclosure 'fold by fold' of his aesthetic world. The work began less ambitiously as a pair of *Improvisations sur Mallarmé* for soprano and percussion ensemble (1957), setting the sonnets 'Le Vierge, le vivace, et le bel aujourd'hui' and 'Une Dentelle s'abolit'. Two years later Boulez added a third *Improvisation*, on the sonnet 'A la Nue accablante tu', for soprano, flutes, trombone, low strings, and large percussion section, and also in 1959 he began *Tombeau* for full orchestra with soprano, based on Mallarmé's sonnet of farewell to Verlaine. The first performance of *Pli selon pli* took place in 1960, with the three *Improvisations* followed by *Tombeau* and preceded by *Don*, essentially a piano piece after Mallarmé's 'Don du poème'. Thus the work made a large-scale crescendo, but Boulez became dissatisfied with this and decided to make the shape symmetrical: in 1962 *Don* was replaced by a new orchestral piece with the same title, and the first *Improvisation* was rescored to balance the third.

It was during the period of work on *Pli selon pli* that Boulez's ideas on the relationships between poetry and music, already of obvious concern in *Le Marteau sans maître*, were developed in a series of articles culminating in 'Poésie—centre et absence—musique' (1962). Here Boulez proposes 'the direct seizure of the poem through music, in the general sphere of form, in syntax, lastly in rhythm and the sound value of the words themselves . . . In short, an amalgamation breaks out through the mediation of structure, this word being understood in its aesthetic and grammatical aspects'. Amalgamation through a correspondence of structure may proceed so far that the text has been displaced: 'The poem, centre of the music, can be absent from it'.

This happens almost completely in the outer movements of *Pli selon pli*, *Don*, and *Tombeau*, which use one of Mallarmé's earliest non-juvenile poems and one of his last. They represent, therefore, the birth and death of the poet, but they stand too for the birth and death of the work of art. The birth in 'Don du poème' is a literary one, specifically that of the dramatic fragment *Hérodiade*, of which the poem contains some foretaste in image and metre. Boulez's *Don* similarly looks forward to the remainder of *Pli selon pli*. After a dedicatory setting of the opening line, the text disappears and the work goes into a state of nascence, of suspended chords, through which prefigurings of the other four sections are drawn to the fore and then lost.

Tombeau is also largely an orchestral work, a gathering accumulation of orchestral groups around the solo piano and also an enormous accelerando which is achieved paradoxically by ever shorter note values in ever slower tempos. Here the voice enters only at the end, called forth almost in desperation by the piano after three previous appeals have failed, and Boulez uses only the last line of the poem: 'A scarce deep rivulet calumniated death.' The imagery and structure of the rest have been subsumed entirely into music; words are needed only to make it clear that the oppressive coming is that of death, and at the close of the work, in a sforzato chord recalling the crack that opened *Don*, there is a Mallarméan assimilation of genesis to extinction.

The first two *Improvisations sur Mallarmé* allow the poem to be present as well as central, and so the transposition of text into music is more readily observed. The process begins with the choice of instrumentation: harp, vibraphone, tubular bells, and unpitched percussion (four players) for the first setting (1957 version), and the same ensemble with the addition of piano and celesta for the second. There is a concentration on sounds of brilliance and long resonance, as throughout much of *Pli selon pli*, in concord with the poetic images of coldness, transparency, whiteness, and reflection. Furthermore, these are sounds which cannot be sustained, which begin to die at the instant of their birth, and in that respect they correspond with the frozen frustration and sterility of which Mallarmé writes.

Those qualities are also present in the vocal writing, of which Ex. 34 shows an example from *Improvisation sur Mallarmé II*:

Ex. 34

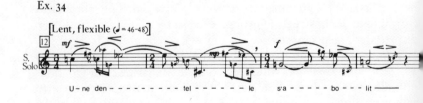

Not only does the line's ornateness make it an almost graphic description of the poem's floating lace curtain, but its restricted pitch repertory contributes a feeling of entrapment. Each note is fixed in register, and the soprano veers wildly, albeit gracefully, within this bounded space. Harmonic limitation of this kind, which can also be found occasionally in *Le Marteau sans maître* (see Ex. 27), is common in *Pli selon pli*, and is largely responsible for Boulez's success in translating so exactly Mallarmé's sense of useless activity.

The other principal vocal style in *Improvisation sur Mallarmé II* is purely syllabic, the soprano singing long notes, in a tempo determined only by her breath, with chords and little figures in the pitched instruments:

Ex. 35

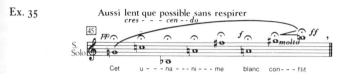

Boulez's use of the two styles, contrasting and then combining them, gives shape to the piece, and that shape is, as one might expect, a reflection of the poetic structure. Ex. 36 gives some indication of how the sonnet emerges in Boulez's treatment: lower-case italic type is used for sections in the decorated manner of Ex. 34, upper-case roman type for syllabic passages, lower-case roman type for decorated music with a tendency to the syllabic, and upper-case italic type for syllabic music with a tendency to the decorated; spacings give an approximation to temporal relations. It is clear that Boulez's setting is attentive not only to the sonnet form and the grammatical construction but also to hidden relations within the poem, such as the correspondence of 'contre le vitre' (line 7) with 'Selon nul ventre' (line 13), or the point of the syllable 'lit' (line 8) to introduce, as a separated word, the gilded dreamer of line 9. One may note, too, that the six emphasized lines make up a new poem containing the essence of the sonnet.

The third *Improvisation sur Mallarmé*, quite distinct in style from the other two, reflects the poetic essence largely in instrumental music and has the most open form to be found in *Pli selon pli*. Here the singer and the players can often choose from two or more supplied variants, and much of the piece is not synchronized exactly. Its heterophonies, together with its percussion scoring (xylophones, vibraphones, harps, celesta, mandolin, and guitar are prominent), slow tempo and use of quarter-tones for soprano and harps, give the movement an oriental air, though the atmosphere is also that of Mallarmé's 'overwhelming cloud' and 'sepulchral shipwreck'.

Ex. 36

une dentelle s'abolit
dans le doute du jeu suprême
à n'entr'ouvrir comme un blasphème

qu'absence éternelle de lit

CET UNANIME BLANC CONFLIT

D'UNE GUIRLANDE   AVEC LA MÊME

ENFUI   CONTRE LA VITRE   BLÊME

FLOT*TE*   *PLUS*   *QU'IL*   *N'EN—*   *SE—*   *VE—*   *LIT*

mais chez *qui du rêve se dore*
tristement   dort une mandore

AU CREUX NÉANT   MUSIC*IEN*

telle que vers quelque fenêtre

SELON NUL VENTRE   *QUE*   *LE*   SIEN

filial on aurait pu   naître

One returns, as always in this work, to Mallarmé, whose verse is so completely its centre. *Improvisation sur Mallarmé II* is not just an expert musical analysis of the sonnet but also an exact mirror to the poetic content, to the connection of potency and sterility, creative abundance and uselessness in the exercise of a solitary sexual act. But further, because the musical assimilation is so complete, the work is independent of Mallarmé: the 'Je' with which it begins has acquired a second author, and *Pli selon pli* is also a portrait of Boulez.

WORK IN PROGRESS

Of the music which he has written since *Pli selon pli*, Boulez has released for publication only one complete work, *Rituel* for orchestra (1974–5), the solo clarinet version of his *Domaines* (1961–8), and two fragments, *Éclat* for fifteen instruments (1965) and the chamber cantata '*Cummings ist der Dichter . . .*' (1970). Each of these fragments is a self-sufficient part of a composition which remains 'work in progress', and it is in this piecemeal fashion that most of Boulez's output has appeared since 1957. *Pli selon pli* grew over a five-year period, and similarly the orchestral *Doubles* (1957–8) was extended in *Figures-Doubles-Prismes* (1963), further expanded in 1968. Other works, like the Third Piano Sonata, appear to have been shelved for a long time: *Domaines* for clarinet and six ensembles, begun in 1961, was not ready for performance until 1968, and the flute solo of *Strophes*, composed in 1957, still awaits its accompaniment of instrumental groups.

Such delays result perhaps from Boulez's method of working: 'As long as my ideas have not exhausted every possibility of proliferation', he has said, 'they stay in my mind.' Moreover, in his aleatory thinking he appears to have moved quickly from the 'fixed mobile' work, created once and for all, to the 'mobile mobile' work, in constant evolution. At the same time, however, his slower creative pace must be attributed in part to his increasing activity as an orchestral conductor, which began in 1956 and steadily developed until, from 1971 to 1975, he was in charge of both the New York Philharmonic and the BBC Symphony Orchestra.

Yet this experience was not without positive effects on his creative work. Very soon, by 1958, he had used his new inside knowledge of the orchestra in revising *Le Soleil des eaux* and in composing two works which use the ensemble in quite original ways, *Doubles* and *Poésie pour pouvoir*. In *Doubles*, or at least in the extended version *Figures-Doubles-Prismes*, the orchestra is divided into fourteen groups, six of strings, three of woodwinds, four of brass, and one of unpitched percussion. These are placed in specified positions on the platform, with several pitched percussion instruments (three harps, celesta, vibraphone, xylophone, and timpani) interspersed among them. As a result Boulez is able to create orchestral sonorities of marvellously fluid variety and astonishing newness, reaching past the models sometimes suggested: Varèse in the 1963 version and Berg in the 1968 addendum. The rich diversity of the score is also a product of its formal process, by which simple initial ideas are developed in variation and interaction; this, rather than the existence of three separate sections, is what the title is meant to suggest.

In *Poésie pour pouvoir* (1958) the new conception of the orchestra is directed by two considerations: the arrangement of the forces in an ascending spiral and the need to integrate live orchestral sound with material on tape, a combination here attempted for the first time. To judge just from a very poor recording of the first and only performance, a connection was established through the percussion, their music merging into and emerging from the clanging electronic sounds. But the tape also includes an element more difficult to assimilate, namely a male voice speaking the long, vitriolic curse by Henri Michaux which gives the work its title. It seems that it was dissatisfaction with the tape that led Boulez to withdraw the piece immediately, and that this experience confirmed his mistrust of electronic means, about which he had had reservations since the time of the *Études*. In 1977, however, after a return to electronics in ' . . . *explosante-fixe* . . . ' (1971–), he spoke of revising *Poésie pour pouvoir* for small and large choruses with live electronics, orchestra, and computer-generated sound on tape.

Meanwhile his exploration of new orchestral possibilities had continued in the four large movements of *Pli selon pli*, each for a different formation, but all giving prominence to an array of pitched percussion instruments. Their use of unpitched percussion is more tentative: it is significant, for example, that the orchestrated version of *Improvisation sur Mallarmé I* curtails the effect of ringing crotales by adding new wind and string counterpoints. One may also note that when, in 1962–4, Boulez sketched a work for percussion ensemble, he gave it the title *Marges*, recalling his comment that the unpitched percussion of *Le Marteau sans maître* are 'marginal'; and that for the next decade he made no use of percussion instruments without pitch.

The reason for this neglect, which parallels Webern's almost throughout his serial music, may be found in Boulez's technical concerns, which were now with the elaboration of a consistent harmonic method, using chord multiplication and register fixing, along lines proposed in *Structures II* and *Pli selon pli*. Unpitched instruments could have no place in music which depended on the investigation, development, and combination of harmonic fields.

Domaines, by its very form, provides clear instances of the new technique in operation: indeed, its rather schematic nature has led Boulez to see a need for substantial revision. The work is scored for solo clarinet and six symmetrically spaced ensembles of stepwise increasing size: a solo bass clarinet, a duo of marimba and pizzicato double bass (preferably electric), a trio of oboe, horn, and electric guitar, a quartet of trombones, a quintet of flute, alto saxophone, trumpet, bassoon, and harp, and a sextet of strings. These groups are always heard in isolation, in antiphony with the soloist. The discourse begins with him playing, in any order, six 'cahiers' marked 'original', each being followed by a corresponding 'cahier' from a particular group. In the second half this arrangement is reversed, so that the groups play their 'miroir' pieces in an order decided by the conductor, each being followed by the relative 'cahier' from the soloist in its 'miroir' version (a slightly varied retrograde of the 'original'). In both parts the clarinettist must move into the neighbourhood, the spatial 'domain', of the group with which he is concerned, and the musical character of the antiphony is made to depend on the relation of sound. For example, the clarinet has most to say to the bass clarinet, and the antiphony is one of figures and shadows. The trio and the quintet are both groups which might readily incorporate the soloist, and their material takes ownership of his. At the other end of the spectrum, the marimba and the bass seem to pursue their own dialogue with ideas suggested by the clarinet.

The 'sixness' of *Domaines* extends to more than the constitution of groups and the number of antiphonies in each part. The solo 'cahiers' (which can be played alone as a solo work) each have six elements which may be linked in different orders, and the music abounds in rhythmic and pitch configurations of six. Ex. 37, one element from 'cahier E' and the ensemble music which immediately follows it in the recording supervised by Boulez, shows several instances of this and demonstrates also how the clarinet's harmonic 'domains' are filled out by the corresponding ensemble:

Ex. 37

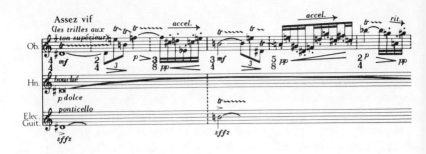

A unit based on six neighbouring notes is stated twice by the clarinet
and imitated by the oboe, which then extends it into a twelve-note
statement. Also, the oboe's triplets are close echoes of the one in the
clarinet part, and the guitar provides an extension of the soloist's
opening interval.

The music for the trio in Ex. 37 is characteristic of *Domaines* in
polarizing around particular pitches, first D♯ as lowest note, then B as
bass and as centrepoint of the oboe's second semiquaver flurry. The
arrival of the high B♭/B trill in the oboe may be felt to provide an
enharmonic dominant on the D♯, though the sense of tonal order in
Boulez's later music depends more generally, as well as in this case
specifically, on the restriction of each different note to a definite
register. By comparison with examples which have been quoted from
Structures I, *Le Marteau sans maître*, *Structures II*, and *Improvisation
sur Mallarmé II*, Ex. 37 shows this technique being used to give an
effect more of gravitation than of fixity.

Phases in the transition can be found in the six-minute *Éclat*, which
has all the lightning brilliance, explosive force, and shimmering
brightness suggested by its title. It might be a description of the swan's
'pur éclat' in 'Le Vierge, le vivace, et le bel aujourd'hui', and this
connection with *Pli selon pli* is not merely poetic: the piece was
developed from the discarded solo piano *Don*, and it takes up from the
scoring for pitched percussion in the Mallarmé portrait, particularly
that in *Improvisation sur Mallarmé II*. There are nine such
instruments—piano, celesta, harp, glockenspiel, vibraphone, mandolin, guitar, cimbalom, and tubular bells—of which only the
cimbalom, which Boulez would have got to know through his
performances of Stravinsky's *Ragtime* and *Renard*, does not appear in
the orchestra of *Pli selon pli*.

Much of *Éclat* is occupied with frenetic trills and nervous
figurations for its scintillating nonet:

Ex. 38

This passage, characteristically, fills out a delimited harmonic field, one of ten different pitches in fixed registers, in a way that contributes much to the static, decorative aspect of such material in the piece. The middle part of the work, marked 'Assez lent, suspendu, comme imprévisible', is quite different, consisting of single events over which the conductor has considerable control in matters of timing and dynamics. Ex. 39 shows the opening sequence of this music, with only pitches and instrumentation indicated:

Ex. 39

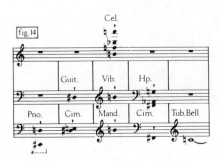

The tubular bell's middle C comes here as a sensed necessity, not only because C is the only pitch not sounded in the first four bars, but also because middle C is almost at the centre of the registral space in use. Later in this slow section, too, harmonic progression is achieved through gradual completions of the chromatic total, though pitch polarization, on the vibraphone's falling major second F#–E, also becomes prominent towards the end. Perhaps, therefore, the music is not so very 'imprévisible', even if suspension is maintained by the lack of tempo and the hanging resonant sounds. It gives the impression, as Boulez has suggested, of an improvisation for the conductor, playing on the keyboard of his ensemble.

Ex. 39 is followed by four similar sequences, increasing then decreasing in complexity and so making a five-part symmetry, albeit disguised, within the larger arch form of *Éclat*: the slow section is surrounded by the embellished music exemplified in Ex. 38, and this in turn is bounded by rhythmically directed material, a piano cadenza at the beginning and a brisk chase of staccato chords in close formation at the end:

Ex. 40

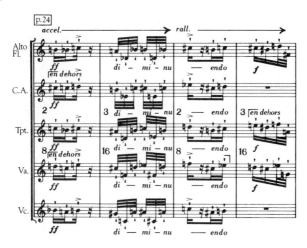

The closing pages effectively introduce the sustaining instruments of the ensemble—alto flute, cor anglais, trumpet, trombone, viola, and cello—which have previously been heard only in a pianissimo chord close to the start. And with their introduction Boulez sets up a contrast between percussive and sustaining instruments, the former associated with single resonating sounds and elaborate figures in a floating tempo, the latter with determined motion. It is this contrast which will provide motivating force as *Éclat* proceeds into *Éclat multiples* (1966–).

The antinomy between fluidity and jerky motion had been exploited in Boulez's music from the time of the First Piano Sonata. That between percussive and sustaining instruments is implicit in much of *Pli selon pli*. *Éclat/multiples*, however, should offer the fullest working out of such contrasts, the conditional being necessary because the work remains incomplete. Its fragmentary first performance, in 1970, showed that the concluding momentum of *Éclat* gives way for a moment in the new section, only to return with renewed vigour when a group of nine violas starts to play. This second section, which also adds a solo basset horn to the ensemble, is to be followed by others, each introducing new instruments, until the percussion nonet is playing against an orchestra of forty-nine.

Boulez has said of *Éclat multiples* that 'the multiple reflections of the original musical images interfere with each other and create divergent perspectives, such as Paul Klee imagined in certain of his paintings'. One of the most extraordinary divergent perspectives is presented within a few minutes, when the added fragment comes up with what sounds like a theme:

Ex. 41

and a theme of an expressive amplitude unparalleled in Boulez's music, unless in the roughly contemporary addition to *Figures-Doubles-Prismes*. This idea is announced by the *Éclat* sustaining sextet in unison, with a change of instrumentation almost for every note, and with alternating decorations of glissandos in the violas and clanging arpeggios in the percussion, so that the two opposed sound characters are reflected across it. (Ex. 41 shows one of two possible rhythms; time signatures have been omitted.)

In fact Ex. 41 is not so much a theme as a melodic quintessence of various features which are to emerge again, more or less clearly, as the music proceeds, these including a straining towards polar pitches. Once again, Ex. 41 is an idea in which registers are fixed, and once again one feels the need for the completion of the chromatic total in the last note. But Ex. 41 also introduces something new to Boulez's harmonic thinking in its open diatonic leanings, and these do not entirely disappear as the work goes on. More typical, however, are its fast and brilliant charges through different spheres of colour and rhythm, among them a long, almost Balinese development in rapid semiquavers, the instrumentation chopped and changed with frantic abandon.

One might regret that Boulez did not continue with *Éclat multiples* rather than launch himself into a new cycle with '*Cummings ist der Dichter . . .*' (1970). This short work, which makes some use of material from the withdrawn *Oubli signal lapidé* (1952), sets a single poem for chamber chorus and small orchestra. It contains several beautiful inventions, such as the free winging of solo woodwind as voices give place to instruments in the latter part, yet its abrupt contrasts of sustained chords with stabs of staccato are strangely bald, and it remains what Boulez has called it, 'an essay'.

If '*Cummings*' suggests an uncertainty of direction, '. . . *explosante-fixe . . .*' may represent another voyage to 'the ends of fruitful land'. The title comes from André Breton—'beauty will be exploding-fixed or it will not be'—and the piece originated as a sort of composition kit, published as one of a number of memorials to Stravinsky in the magazine *Tempo*. Basic melodic-rhythmic material is provided in the form of an 'originel' (the adjectival ending has become more definite since *Domaines*) and six planetary 'transitoires', the 'originel' being a decorated E♭ (in German, 'Es', for Stravinsky) and the 'transitoires' containing more varied ideas. The musical text is accompanied by several pages of notes, explaining how this material may be used in a more or less free composition for any number of musicians.

Boulez's own realization, begun in 1972, develops the given ideas and assigns them to seven musical characters—flute, clarinet, trumpet, violin, viola, cello, and harp plus vibraphone—who proceed through their fully notated 'originels' and 'transitoires' along separate paths, all joining together in the final section. Each part is limited almost exclusively to a fixed set of twelve chromatic pitches, each set being a transposition of every other. Ex. 42 shows, for example, part of the 'originel' material for the flute and the violin, as used at the performance in Rome in 1973 (the music has been several times revised, but the essentials remain the same):

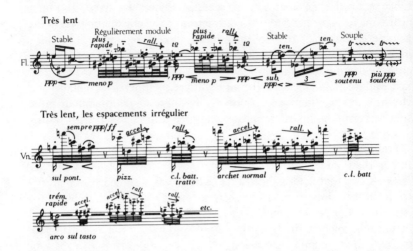

'. . . *explosante-fixe* . . .' thus presents itself as a work of obsessive reiteration and return, each character pursuing a solitary path through a bleak musical landscape, each boxed into its ungenerous harmonic space. The separation of the ensemble is complete, and yet it appears that Boulez does not intend it so. Live electronic equipment is meant to produce 'an interaction of the parts among themselves' and to 'transform the individual quality of a "natural" sound into a neutral collectivity of "artificial" sounds'. So far these aims have not been achieved, and the piece remains a priority in Boulez's research at the Institut de Recherche et Coordination Acoustique/Musique (IRCAM) in Paris, of which he took full-time charge as director in 1977.

The fixedness of '. . . *explosante-fixe* . . .' is transferred to another plane in a second memorial piece, *Rituel* for orchestra (1974–5), which Boulez wrote as an epitaph for Bruno Maderna. Here he imposes extraordinary restrictions not only on register but also on formal shape and harmonic variety. The work is, in Boulez's appropriately liturgical terms, a sequence of 'verses and refrains', the former consisting of unsynchronized heterophonies of orchestral groups, the latter largely of immense chords. As in *Domaines*, the orchestra is divided into ensembles of diverse sizes, but now the number seven is dominant. Solo oboe, clarinet duo, flute trio, violin quartet, woodwind quintet, string sextet, woodwind heptet, and a group of fourteen brass are each accompanied by a percussion player (two for the brass), whose function is mainly to beat out time on unpitched instruments. As the work proceeds, so, more or less, the number of groups in play increases, until the whole ensemble is locked into chords in the long coda, this bringing a gradual harmonic and instrumental dissolution.

The awesome grandeur of *Rituel* depends not only on its severe structure but also on its obsession with a single kind of harmony, one containing three tritone pairs and another note (again seven) within the interval of a perfect twelfth. Ex. 43 shows the first verse, which announces the 'formula':

Ex. 43

This is extended, developed, rearranged, and transposed (each instrumental group has its own set of transpositions) in each succeeding verse, but the identity is never in doubt. The refrains, of which Ex. 44 provides an example, are based on the inversion of the formula set, and this remains always the same, though transposed, always dissolving in steps. These chords were played synchronously at the première, but in a 1977 performance Boulez eased their monumental character by staggering the entries of instrumental groups throughout the refrain sections.

It is possible that *Rituel* will come to be seen, in the context of future compositions, as an extreme and untypically austere instance of the

later Boulez's derivation of whole works from a few basic harmonic ideas. His next piece, *Messagesquisse* for cello solo and six other cellos (1976), is also based on a formula, that obtained from the name of (Paul) Sacher, but this is an ebullient virtuoso work which makes some

return in the direction of *Éclat multiples*. Whether or not it is extended, as Boulez has proposed, into a 'concerto for orchestra', it seems likely that his creative development will be linked less with the concert podium than with the research laboratories of IRCAM.

LIST OF WORKS

MANY of Boulez's works have appeared in print only some years after their composition, and so it has seemed useful to give copyright dates, these appearing immediately after the name of the publisher.

Notations for piano, 1945, withdrawn

Trois psalmodies for piano, 1945, withdrawn

Variations for piano left hand, 1945, withdrawn

Quartet for four ondes martenot, 1945–6, withdrawn
   recomposed as Sonata for two pianos, 1948, withdrawn

Sonatina for flute and piano, 1946 (Amphion, 1954)

Piano Sonata No. 1, 1946 (Amphion, 1951)

Le Visage nuptial (Char) for soprano, contralto, two ondes martenot, piano, and percussion, 1946–7
   revised for soprano, contralto, women's chorus, and large orchestra, 1951–2 (Heugel, 1959)

Symphonie concertante for piano and orchestra, 1947, lost

Piano Sonata No. 2, 1947–8 (Heugel, 1950; Mercury, 1950)

Le Soleil des eaux (Char, music for radio play) for voices and orchestra, 1948
   extracts revised as concert work for soprano, tenor, bass, and orchestra, 1948, withdrawn
   revised for soprano, tenor, bass, STB chorus, and orchestra, 1958 (Heugel, 1959)
   revised for soprano, SATB chorus, and orchestra, 1965 (Heugel, 1968)

Livre pour quatuor for string quartet, 1948–9 (Heugel, 1960, omitting IV and VI), withdrawn
   recomposed as *Livre pour cordes* for large string orchestra, 1968 (Ia. Variation, Ib. Mouvement), other sections in progress

Polyphonie X for eighteen instruments, 1951, withdrawn
   revision in progress

Étude sur un son and *Étude sur sept sons* on single-track tape, 1951–2

Structures for two pianos, first book, 1951–2 (Universal, 1955)

Oubli signal lapidé (Gatti) for twelve voices, 1952, withdrawn

Le Marteau sans maître (Char) for contralto, alto flute, xylorimba, vibraphone, percussion, guitar, and viola, 1953–5 (Universal, 1954)
   revised in 1957 (Universal, 1957; Philharmonia, 1976)

Orestie (Aeschylus/Claudel, music for stage play) for voices and instrumental ensemble, 1955

Symphonie mécanique (music for film) on single-track tape, 1955

Piano Sonata No. 3, 1956–7, in five formants:
  Antiphonie (fragment *Sigle*, Universal, 1968), revision in progress
  Trope (Universal, 1961)
  Constellation (retrograde version *Constellation-Miroir*, Universal, 1963)
  Strophe, revision in progress
  Séquence, revision in progress

Structures for two pianos, second book, 1956–61 (Universal, 1967)

Le Crépuscule de Yang Koueï-fei (Louise Fauré, music for radio play), 1957

Strophes for flute, 1957, intended to have accompaniment for instrumental groups

Improvisation sur Mallarmé I : Le Vierge, le vivace, et le bel aujourd' hui [= *Pli selon pli*
  II] for soprano, harp, vibraphone, tubular bells, and four percussion, 1957
  (Universal, 1958)
  alternative version for soprano and small orchestra, 1962 (Universal, 1977)

Improvisation sur Mallarmé II : Une Dentelle s'abolit [= *Pli selon pli* III] for soprano,
  harp, vibraphone, piano, celesta, tubular bells, and four percussion, 1957
  (Universal, 1958)

Doubles for large orchestra, 1957–8
  expanded as *Figures-Doubles-Prismes* for large orchestra, 1963
  new section added, 1968

Poésie pour pouvoir (Michaux) for five-track tape and orchestra, 1958, withdrawn

Improvisation sur Mallarmé III : A la Nue accablante tu [= *Pli selon pli* IV] for soprano
  and small orchestra, 1959

Tombeau [= *Pli selon pli* V] (Mallarmé) for soprano and orchestra, 1959–62
  (Universal, 1971)

Don [= *Pli selon pli* I] (Mallarmé) for soprano and piano, 1960, withdrawn
  new work for soprano and orchestra, 1962 (Universal, 1967)

Domaines for clarinet with or without twenty-one instruments in six groups, 1961-8
  revised in 1969 (clarinet solo, Universal, 1970)

Marges for percussion ensemble, 1962–4, sketches only

Éclat for nine percussion and six other instruments, 1965 (Universal, 1965)
  expanded as *Éclat multiples* for nine percussion and orchestra, 1966–, fragment
  performed in 1970

Untitled contribution to *A Garland for Dr. K.* for flute, clarinet, viola, cello, and piano,
  1969

'*Cummings ist der Dichter . . .*' for chamber chorus and small orchestra, 1970
  (Universal, 1976)

'*. . . explosante-fixe . . .*' for variable forces, 1971 (Universal, 1971, in *Tempo* magazine)
  realized for flute, clarinet, harp, vibraphone, trumpet, violin, viola, cello, and
  electronics, 1972–, various versions performed since 1972

Ainsi parla Zarathoustra (Nietzsche/Barrault, music for stage play) for voices and
  instrumental ensemble, 1974

Rituel for orchestra in eight groups, 1974–5 (Universal, 1975)

Messagesquisse for solo cello and six other cellos, 1976

Writings by Boulez

Boulez's writings far outnumber his compositions. They range from polemical squibs to searching analyses, from programme notes to essays on aesthetics, from outlines of compositional technique to ruminations on the music of others. A fair amount of his literary output is contained in the following volumes:

Penser la musique aujourd'hui (Paris, Gonthier, 1963), Eng. trans. as *Boulez on Music Today* (London, Faber, 1971)

Relevés d'apprenti (Paris, Seuil, 1966), Eng. trans. as *Notes of an Apprenticeship* (New York, Knopf, 1968)

Werkstatt-Texte (Frankfurt and Berlin, Propyläen, 1972)

Anhaltspunkte (Stuttgart and Zurich, Belser, 1975)

Par Volonté et par hasard: entretiens avec Célestin Deliège (Paris, Seuil, 1975), Eng. trans. as *Conversations with Célestin Deliège* (London, Eulenburg, 1977)

The following list includes the most important articles on compositional technique which have appeared in English other than in *Notes of an Apprenticeship*:

'"At the ends of fruitful land..."', *Die Reihe*, No. 1 (1958), pp. 19–29

'"Sonata, que me veux-tu?"', *Perspectives of New Music*, Vol. 1, No. 2 (1963), pp. 32–44

'Aléa', *Perspectives of New Music*, Vol. 3, No. 1 (1964), pp. 42–53

'Technology and the Composer', *Times Literary Supplement* (6 May 1977), pp. 570–1

Writings on Boulez

Jean Barraqué: 'Rythme et développement', *Polyphonie*, No. 9–10 (1954), pp. 47–73

Antoine Goléa: *Rencontres avec Pierre Boulez* (Paris, Julliard, 1958)

György Ligeti: 'Pierre Boulez: Entscheidung und Automatik in der Structure IA', *Die Reihe*, No. 4 (1958), pp. 33ff; Eng. trans. in *Die Reihe*, No. 4 (1960), pp. 36–62

Marc Wilkinson: 'Pierre Boulez' Structure Ia: Some Thoughts on Twelve-tone Method', *Gravesaner Blätter*, No. 10 (1958), pp. 23ff

Karlheinz Stockhausen: 'Musik und Sprache', *Die Reihe*, No. 5 (1960), pp. 36ff; Eng. trans. in *Die Reihe*, No. 6 (1964), pp. 40–64

Michel Butor: 'Mallarmé selon Boulez', *Melos*, Vol. 28 (1961), pp. 356ff

André Hodeir: *La Musique depuis Debussy* (Paris, P.U.F., 1961), pp. 104–38

G. W. Hopkins: 'Le Soleil des eaux', *Tempo*, No. 68 (1964), pp. 35ff

Konrad Boehmer: *Zur Theorie der offenen Form in der neuen Musik* (Darmstadt, 1967), pp. 84ff

G. W. Hopkins: 'Debussy and Boulez', *The Musical Times*, Vol. 109 (1968), pp. 710ff

Jean-Pierre Derrien: 'Dossier: Pierre Boulez', *Musique en jeu*, No. 1 (1970), pp. 103–32

Iwanka Stoïanowa: 'Pli selon pli: portrait de Mallarmé', *Musique en jeu*, No. 11 (1973), pp. 75–98

R. Gehrlach: 'Pierre Boulez und Stéphane Mallarmé: ein Fragment über das Artifizielle', *Über Musik und Sprache*, ed. R. Stephan (Mainz, Schott, 1974), pp. 70ff

Iwanka Stoïanowa: 'La Troisième Sonate de Boulez et le projet mallarméen du livre', *Musique en jeu*, No. 16 (1974), pp. 9–28

Iwanka Stoïanowa: 'Verbe et son "centre et absence"', *Musique en jeu* No. 16 (1974), pp. 79–102